D1287211

SONGS OF THE SEA

Books by Rudyard Kipling

Actions and Reactions
Brushwood Boy, The
Captains Courageous
Collected Verse
Day's Work, The
Debits and Credits
Departmental Ditties and Ballads and Barrack-Room Ballads
Diversity of Creatures, A
Eyes of Asia, The
Feet of the Young Men, The
Five Nations, The
France at War
Fringes of the Fleet
From Sea to Sea
History of England, A
Independence
Irish Guards in the Great War, The
Jungle Book, The
Jungle Book, Second
Just So Song Book
Just So Stories
Kim
Kipling Anthology, A Prose and Verse
Kipling Stories and Poems Every Child Should Know
Kipling Birthday Book, The
Land and Sea Tales
Letters of Travel
Life's Handicap: Being Stories of Mine Own People
Light That Failed, The
Many Inventions
Naulahka, The (With Wolcott Balestier)
Plain Tales From the Hills
Puck of Pook's Hill
Rewards and Fairies
Rudyard Kipling's Verse: Inclusive Edition, 1885-1918
Sea and Sussex
Sea Warfare
Seven Seas, The
Soldier Stories
Soldiers Three, The Story of the Gadsbys, and In Black and White
Song of the English, A
Songs for Youth
Songs From Books
Songs of the Sea
Stalky & Co.
They
Traffics and Discoveries
Two Jungle Books, The
Under the Deodars, The Phantom 'Rickshaw, and Wee Willie Winkie
With the Night Mail
Years Between, The

SONGS OF THE SEA

FROM

RUDYARD KIPLING'S VERSE

Illustrated by
DONALD MAXWELL

DOUBLEDAY, PAGE & COMPANY
GARDEN CITY NEW YORK
1927

FIRST EDITION

CONTENTS

LIST OF ILLUSTRATIONS

LIST OF ILLUSTRATIONS—*continued.*

LIST OF ILLUSTRATIONS—*continued.*

LIST OF ILLUSTRATIONS—*continued.*

INDEX TO FIRST LINES OF VERSES

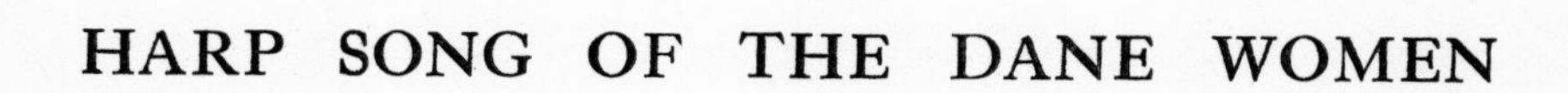

HARP SONG OF THE DANE WOMEN

HARP SONG OF THE DANE WOMEN

What is a woman that you forsake her,
And the hearth-fire and the home-acre,
To go with the old grey Widow-maker?

She has no house to lay a guest in—
But one chill bed for all to rest in,
That the pale suns and the stray bergs nest in.

SONGS OF THE SEA

She has no strong white arms to fold you,
But the ten-times-fingering weed to hold you—
Out on the rocks where the tide has rolled you.

Yet, when the signs of summer thicken,
And the ice breaks, and the birch-buds quicken,
Yearly you turn from our side, and sicken—

Sicken again for the shouts and the slaughters.
You steal away to the lapping waters,
And look at your ship in her winter quarters.

You forget our mirth, and talk at the tables,
The kine in the shed and the horse in the stables—
To pitch her sides and go over her cables.

Then you drive out where the storm-clouds swallow,
And the sound of your oar-blades, falling hollow,
Is all we have left through the months to follow.

You steal away to the lapping waters,
And look at your ship in her winter quarters.

Printed in Great Britain

HARP SONG OF THE DANE WOMEN

Ah, what is woman that you forsake her,
And the hearth-fire and the home-acre,
To go with the old grey Widow-maker?

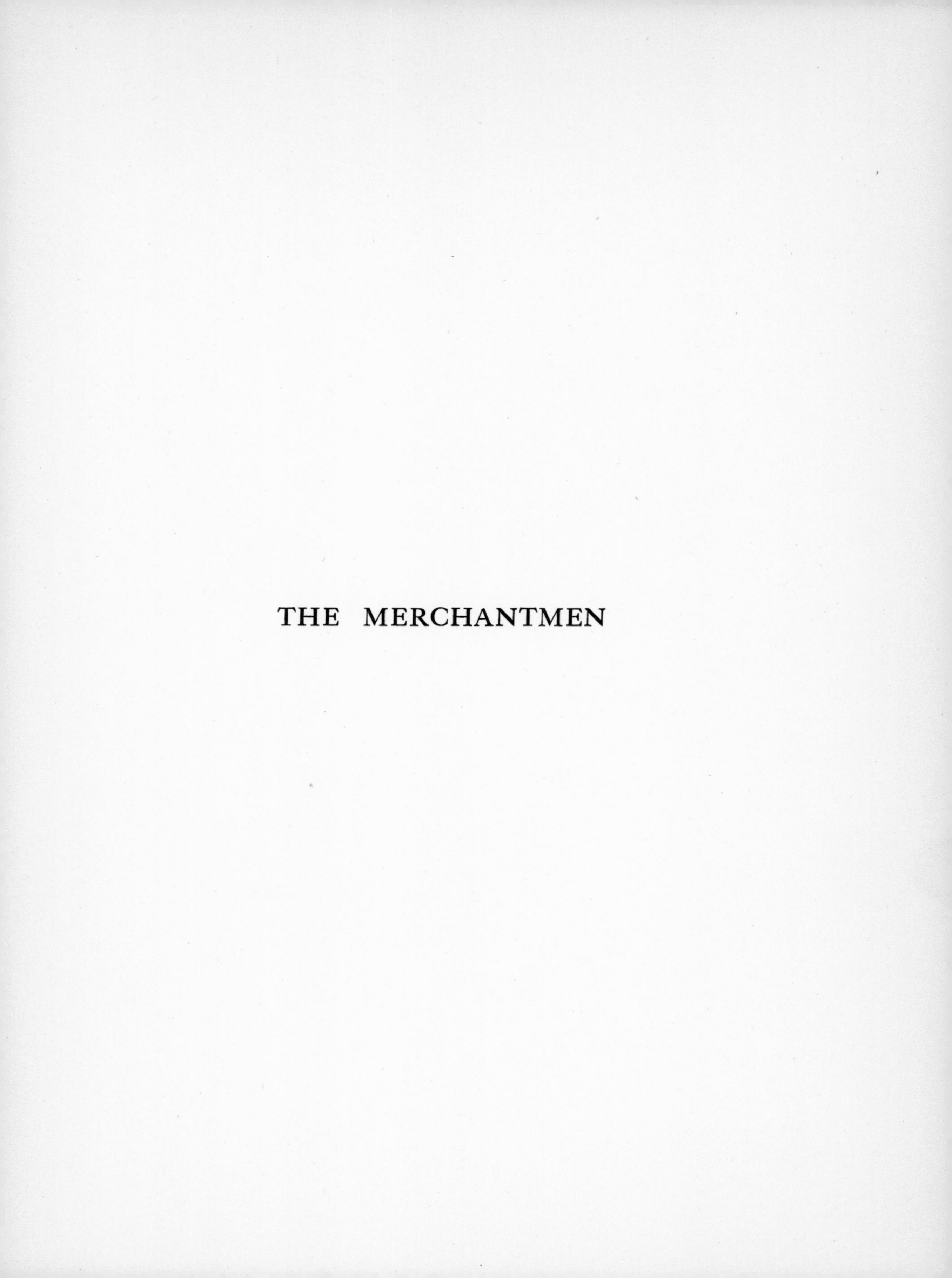

THE MERCHANTMEN

THE MERCHANTMEN

King Solomon drew merchantmen,
  Because of his desire
For peacocks, apes, and ivory,
  From Tarshish unto Tyre:
With cedars out of Lebanon
  Which Hiram rafted down,
But we be only sailormen
  That use in London town.

Coastwise—cross-seas—round the world and back again—
  Where the flaw shall head us or the full Trade suits—
Plain-sail—storm-sail—lay your board and tack again—
  And that's the way we'll pay Paddy Doyle for his boots!

We bring no store of ingots,
  Of spice or precious stones,
But that we have we gathered
  With sweat and aching bones:
In flame beneath the tropics,
  In frost upon the floe,
And jeopardy of every wind
  That does between them go.

And some we got by purchase,
  And some we had by trade,
And some we found by courtesy
  Of pike and carronade—
At midnight, 'mid-sea meetings,
  For charity to keep,
And light the rolling homeward-bound
  That rode a foot too deep.

By sport of bitter weather
  We're walty, strained, and scarred
From the kentledge on the kelson
  To the slings upon the yard.
Six oceans had their will of us
  To carry all away—
Our galley's in the Baltic,
  And our boom's in Mossel Bay!

Beyond all outer charting
We sailed where none have sailed,
And saw the land-lights burning
On islands none have hailed ;
Our hair stood up for wonder,
But, when the night was done,
There danced the deep to windward
Blue-empty 'neath the sun !

Printed in Great Britain

THE MERCHANTMEN

We've floundered off the Texel,
  Awash with sodden deals,
We've slipped from Valparaiso
  With the Norther at our heels:
We've ratched beyond the Crossets
  That tusk the Southern Pole,
And dipped our gunnels under
  To the dread Agulhas roll.

Beyond all outer charting
  We sailed where none have sailed,
And saw the land-lights burning
  On islands none have hailed;
Our hair stood up for wonder,
  But, when the night was done,
There danced the deep to windward
  Blue-empty 'neath the sun!

Strange consorts rode beside us
  And brought us evil luck;
The witch-fire climbed our channels,
  And flared on vane and truck:
Till, through the red tornado,
  That lashed us nigh to blind,
We saw The Dutchman plunging,
  Full canvas, head to wind!

We've heard the Midnight Leadsman
  That calls the black deep down—
Ay, thrice we've heard The Swimmer,
  The Thing that may not drown.
On frozen bunt and gasket
  The sleet-cloud drave her hosts,
When, manned by more than signed
    with us,
  We passed the Isle o' Ghosts!

And north, amid the hummocks,
  A biscuit-toss below,
We met the silent shallop
  That frighted whalers know;
For, down a cruel ice-lane,
  That opened as he sped,
We saw dead Henry Hudson
  Steer, North by West, his dead.

So dealt God's waters with us
  Beneath the roaring skies,
So walked His signs and marvels
  All naked to our eyes:
But we were heading homeward
  With trade to lose or make—
Good Lord, they slipped behind us
  In the tailing of our wake!

THE MERCHANTMEN

Let go, let go the anchors;
  Now shamed at heart are we
To bring so poor a cargo home
  That had for gift the sea!
Let go the great bow-anchors—
  Ah, fools were we and blind—
The worst we stored with utter toil,
  The best we left behind!

Coastwise—cross-seas—round the world and back again,
  Whither flaw shall fail us or the Trades drive down:
Plain-sail—storm-sail—lay your board and tack again—
  And all to bring a cargo up to London Town!

THE WET LITANY

THE WET LITANY

When the water's countenance
Blurrs 'twixt glance and second glance;
When our tattered smokes forerun,
Ashen 'neath a silvered sun;
When the curtain of the haze
Shuts upon our helpless ways—
  Hear the Channel Fleet at sea;
  Libera nos Domine!

When the engines' bated pulse
Scarcely thrills the nosing hulls;
When the wash along the side
Sounds, a sudden, magnified;
When the intolerable blast
Marks each blindfold minute passed;

When the fog-buoy's squattering flight
Guides us through the haggard night;
When the warning bugle blows;
When the lettered doorways close;
When our brittle townships press,
Impotent, on emptiness;

When the unseen leadsmen lean
Questioning a deep unseen;
When their lessened count they tell
To a bridge invisible;
When the hid and perilous
Cliffs return our cry to us;

When the treble thickness spread
Swallows up our next-ahead;
When her siren's frightened whine
Shows her sheering out of line;
When, her passage undiscerned,
We must turn where she has turned,
  Hear the Channel Fleet at sea;
  Libera nos Domine!

When our tattered smokes forerun,
Ashen 'neath a silvered sun ;
When the curtain of the haze
Shuts upon our helpless ways—
  Hear the Channel Fleet at sea ;
  Libera nos Domine !

Printed in Great Britain

THE SONG OF DIEGO VALDEZ

THE SONG OF DIEGO VALDEZ

The God of Fair Beginnings
  Hath prospered here my hand—
The cargoes of my lading,
  And the keels of my command.
For out of many ventures
  That sailed with hope as high,
My own have made the better trade,
  And Admiral am I!

To me my King's much honour,
  To me my people's love—
To me the pride of Princes
  And power all pride above;
To me the shouting cities,
  To me the mob's refrain:—
'Who knows not noble Valdez,
  Hath never heard of Spain.'

But I remember comrades—
  Old playmates on new seas—
Whenas we traded orpiment
  Among the savages—
A thousand leagues to south'ard
  And thirty years removed—
They know not noble Valdez,
  But me they knew and loved.

Then they that found good liquor,
  They drank it not alone,
And they that found fair plunder,
  They told us every one,
About our chosen islands
  Or secret shoals between,
When, walty from far voyage,
  We gathered to careen.

To me the shouting cities,
  To me the mob's refrain :—
' Who knows not noble Valdez,
  Hath never heard of Spain.'

Printed in Great Britain

THE SONG OF DIEGO VALDEZ

They burned our breaming-fagots
  All pale along the shore:
There rose our worn pavilions—
  A sail above an oar:
As flashed each yearning anchor
  Through mellow seas afire,
So swift our careless captains
  Rowed each to his desire.

Where lay our loosened harness?
  Where turned our naked feet?
Whose tavern 'mid the palm-trees?
  What quenchings of what heat?
Oh fountain in the desert!
  Oh cistern in the waste!
Oh bread we ate in secret!
  Oh cup we spilled in haste!

The youth new-taught of longing,
  The widow curbed and wan—
The goodwife proud at season,
  And the maid aware of man;
All souls unslaked, consuming,
  Defrauded in delays,
Desire not more their quittance
  Than I those forfeit days!

I dreamed to wait my pleasure
  Unchanged my spring would bide:
Wherefore, to wait my pleasure,
  I put my spring aside
Till, first in face of Fortune,
  And last in mazed disdain,
I made Diego Valdez
  High Admiral of Spain.

Then walked no wind 'neath Heaven
  Nor surge that did not aid—
I dared extreme occasion,
  Nor ever one betrayed.
They wrought a deeper treason—
  (Led seas that served my needs!)
They sold Diego Valdez
  To bondage of great deeds.

The tempest flung me seaward,
  And pinned and bade me hold
The course I might not alter—
  And men esteemed me bold!
The calms embayed my quarry,
  The fog-wreath sealed his eyes;
The dawn-wind brought my topsails—
  And men esteemed me wise!

THE SONG OF DIEGO VALDEZ

Yet 'spite my tyrant triumphs
  Bewildered, dispossessed—
My dream held I before me—
  My vision of my rest;
But, crowned by Fleet and People,
  And bound by King and Pope—
Stands here Diego Valdez
  To rob me of my hope!

No prayer of mine shall move him,
  No word of his set free
The Lord of Sixty Pennants
  And the Steward of the Sea.
His will can loose ten thousand
  To seek their loves again—
But not Diego Valdez,
  High Admiral of Spain.

There walks no wind 'neath Heaven
  Nor wave that shall restore
The old careening riot
  And the clamorous, crowded shore—
The fountain in the desert,
  The cistern in the waste,
The bread we ate in secret,
  The cup we spilled in haste!

Now call I to my Captains—
  For council fly the sign,
Now leap their zealous galleys
  Twelve-oared across the brine.
To me the straiter prison,
  To me the heavier chain—
To me Diego Valdez,
  High Admiral of Spain.

THE LINER SHE'S A LADY

THE LINER SHE'S A LADY

The Liner she's a lady, an' she never looks nor 'eeds—
The Man-o'-War's 'er 'usband, an' 'e gives 'er all she needs;
But, oh, the little cargo-boats, that sail the wet seas roun',
They're just the same as you an' me a-plyin' up an' down!

Plyin' up an' down, Jenny, 'angin' round the Yard,
All the way by Fratton tram down to Portsmouth 'Ard;
Anythin' for business, an' we're growin' old—
Plyin' up an' down, Jenny, waitin' in the cold!

The Liner she's a lady by the paint upon 'er face,
An' if she meets an accident they count it sore disgrace:
The Man-o'-War's 'er 'usband, and 'e's always 'andy by,
But, oh, the little cargo-boats! they've got to load or die.

The Liner she's a lady, and 'er route is cut an' dried;
The Man-o'-War's 'er 'usband, an' 'e always keeps beside;
But, oh, the little cargo-boats that 'aven't any man,
They've got to do their business first, and make the most they can!

The Liner she's a lady, and if a war should come,
The Man-o'-War's 'er 'usband, and 'e'd bid 'er stay at home;
But, oh, the little cargo-boats that fill with every tide!
'E'd 'ave to up an' fight for them, for they are England's pride.

The Liner she's a lady, an' she never looks nor 'eeds—
The Man-'o-War's 'er 'usband, an' 'e gives 'er all she needs ;
But, oh, the little cargo-boats, that sail the wet seas roun',
They're just the same as you an' me a'plyin' up an' down.

Printed in Great Britain

THE LINER SHE'S A LADY

The Liner she's a lady, but if she wasn't made,
There still would be the cargo-boats for 'ome an' foreign trade,
The Man-o'-War's 'er 'usband, but if we wasn't 'ere,
'E wouldn't have to fight at all for 'ome an' friends so dear.

'Ome an' friends so dear, Jenny, 'angin' round the Yard,
All the way by Fratton tram down to Portsmouth 'Ard;
Anythin' for business, an' we're growin' old—
'Ome an' friends so dear, Jenny, waitin' in the cold!

THE JUNK AND THE DHOW

THE JUNK AND THE DHOW

Once a pair of savages found a stranded tree.
  (*One-piecee stick-pidgin—two-piecee man.*
Straddle-um—paddle-um—push-um off to sea,
  That way Foleign Devil-boat began.[1])
But before, and before, and ever so long before
  Any shape of sailing-craft was known,
The Junk and Dhow had a stern and a bow,
  And a mast and a sail of their own—alone, alone!
  As they crashed across the Oceans on their own!

[1]Remember, the Chinaman generally says "l" for "r."

Once there was a pirate-ship, being blown ashore—
(*Plitty soon pilum up, s'posee no can tack.*
Seven-piecee stlong man pullum sta'boa'd oar.
That way bling her head alound and sail-o back.)
But before, and before, and ever so long before
Grand Commander Noah took the wheel,
The Junk and the Dhow, though they look like any-how,
Had rudders reaching deep below their keel—akeel—akeel!
As they laid the Eastern Seas beneath their keel!

Once there was a galliot yawing in a tide.
(*Too much foolee side-slip. How can stop?*
Man catchee tea-box lid—lasha longaside.
That way make her plenty glip and sail first-chop.)
But before, and before, and ever so long before
Any such contrivances were used,
The whole Confucian sea-board had standardized the lee-board,
And hauled it up or dropped it as they choosed—or chose—or choosed!
According to the weather, when they cruised!

But before, and before, and ever so long before
Grand Commander Noah took the wheel,
The Junk and the Dhow, though they look like anyhow,
Had rudders reaching deep below their keel—akeel—akeel !
As they laid the Eastern Seas beneath their keel.

Printed in Great Britain

THE JUNK AND THE DHOW

Once there was a caravel in a beam-sea roll—
  (*Cargo shiftee—alla dliftee—no can livee long.*
S'posum' nail-o boa'd acloss—makee ploper hol'?
  That way, cargo sittum still, and ship mo' stlong.)
But before, and before, and ever so long before
  Any square-rigged vessel hove in sight
The Canton deep-sea craft carried bulkheads fore and
    aft,
  And took good care to keep 'em water-tight—atite—
    atite!
  From Amboyna to the Great Australian Bight!

Once there was a sailor-man singing just this way—
  (*Too muchee yowl-o, sickum best flend!*
Singee all-same pullee lope—haul and belay.
  Hully up and coilum down an'—bite off end!)
But before, and before, and ever so long before
  Any sort of chanty crossed our lips,
The Junk and the Dhow, though they look like any-
    how,
  Were the Mother and the Father of all Ships—
    ahoy!—aships!
  And of half the new inventions in our ships!

From Tarifa to Formosa of our Ships!
From Socotra to Sel*ank*hor of the windlass and the anchor,
And the Navigators' Compass on our Ships—ahoy!—our Ships!
(*O, hully up and coilum down and bite off end!*)

CRUISERS

CRUISERS

As our mother the Frigate, bepainted and fine,
Made play for her bully the Ship of the Line;
So we, her bold daughters by iron and fire,
Accost and decoy to our masters' desire.

Now pray you consider what toils we endure,
Night-walking wet sea-lanes, a guard and a lure;
Since half of our trade is that same pretty sort
As mettlesome wenches do practise in port.

For this is our office: to spy and make room
As hiding yet guiding the foe to their doom;
Surrounding, confounding, to bait and betray
And tempt them to battle the seas' width away.

The pot-bellied merchant foreboding no wrong
With headlight and sidelight he lieth along,
Till, lightless and lightfoot and lurking, leap we
To force him discover his business by sea.

And when we have wakened the lust of a foe,
To draw him by flight toward our bullies we go,
Till, 'ware of strange smoke stealing nearer, he flies—
Or our bullies close in for to make him good prize.

So, when we have spied on the path of their host,
One flieth to carry that word to the coast;
And, lest by false doubling they turn and go free,
One lieth behind them to follow and see.

The pot-bellied merchant foreboding no wrong
With headlight and sidelight he lieth along,
Till, lightless and lightfoot and lurking, leap we
To force him discover his business by sea.

CRUISERS

Anon we return, being gathered again,
Across the sad valleys all drabbled with rain—
Across the grey ridges all crispèd and curled—
To join the long dance round the curve of the world.

The bitter salt spindrift: the sun-glare likewise:
The moon-track a-quiver bewilders our eyes,
Where, linking and lifting, our sisters we hail
'Twixt wrench of cross-surges or plunge of head-gale.

As maidens awaiting the bride to come forth
Make play with light jestings and wit of no worth,
So, widdershins circling the bride-bed of Death,
Each fleereth her neighbour and signeth and saith:—

'What see ye? Their signals, or levin afar?
'What hear ye? God's thunder, or guns of our war?
'What mark ye? Their smoke, or the cloud-rack out-
blown?
'What chase ye? Their lights, or the Daystar low
down?'

So, times past all number deceived by false shows,
Deceiving we cumber the road of our foes,
For this is our virtue—to track and betray;
Preparing great battles a sea's width away.

Now peace is at end and our peoples take heart,
For the laws are clean gone that restrained our art;
Up and down the near headlands and against the far wind
We are loosed (O be swift!) to the work of our kind!

THE NURSES

THE NURSES

When, with a pain he desires to explain to the multitude, Baby
Howls himself black in the face, toothlessly striving to curse;
And the six-months-old Mother begins to enquire of the Gods if it may be
Tummy, or Temper, or Pins—what does the adequate Nurse?

See! At one turn of her head the trouble is guessed; and, thereafter,
She juggles (unscared by his throes) with drops of hot water and spoons,
Till the hiccoughs are broken by smiles, and the smiles pucker up into laughter,
And he lies o'er her shoulder and crows, and she, as she nurses him, croons!

When, at the head of the grade, tumultuous out of the cutting,
Pours the belated Express, roars at the night, and draws clear,
Redly obscured or displayed by her fire-door's opening and shutting—
Symbol of strength under stress—what does her small engineer?

Clamour and darkness encircle his way. Do they deafen or blind him?
No!—nor the pace he must keep. He, being used to these things,
Placidly follows his work, which is laying his mileage behind him,
While his passengers trustfully sleep, and he, as he handles her, sings!

Clamour and darkness encircle his way. Do they deafen or blind him ?
No !—nor the pace he must keep.

Printed in Great Britain

THE NURSES

When, with the gale at her heel, the barque lies down
and recovers—
Rolling through forty degrees, combing the stars with
her tops—
What says the man at the wheel, holding her straight
as she hovers
On the summits of wind-screening seas, steadying her
as she drops?

Behind him the blasts without check from the Pole to
the Tropic, pursue him,
Heaving up, heaping high, slamming home, the surges
he must not regard:
Beneath him the crazy wet deck, and all Ocean on end
to undo him;
Above him one desperate sail, thrice-reefed but still
buckling the yard!

Under his hand fleet the spokes and return, to be held
or set free again;
And she bows and makes shift to obey their behest,
till the master-wave comes,
And her gunnel goes under in thunder and smokes,
and she chokes in the trough of the sea again—
Ere she can lift and make way to its crest; and he, as
he nurses her, hums!

These have so utterly mastered their work that they work without thinking;
Holding three-fifths of their brain in reserve for whatever betide.
So, when catastrophe threatens, of colic, collision or sinking,
They shunt the full gear into train, and take that small thing in their stride.

SONG OF THE RED WAR-BOAT
(A.D. 683)

SONG OF THE RED WAR-BOAT
(A.D. 683)

Shove off from the wharf-edge! Steady!
Watch for a smooth! Give way!
If she feels the lop already
She'll stand on her head in the bay.
It's ebb—it's dusk—it's blowing,
The shoals are a mile of white,
But (snatch her along!) we're going
To find our master to-night.

For we hold that in all disaster
Of shipwreck, storm, or sword,
A Man must stand by his Master
When once he has pledged his word.

Raging seas have we rowed in,
But we seldom saw them thus:
Our master is angry with Odin—
Odin is angry with us!
Heavy odds have we taken,
But never before such odds.
The Gods know they are forsaken,
We must risk the wrath of the Gods.

Over the crest she flies from,
Into its hollow she drops,
Cringes and clears her eyes from
The wind-torn breaker-tops,
Ere out on the shrieking shoulder
Of a hill-high surge she drives.
Meet her! Meet her and hold her!
Pull for your scoundrel lives!

The thunders bellow and clamour
The harm that they mean to do!
There goes Thor's own Hammer
Cracking the dark in two!
Close! But the blow has missed her,
Here comes the wind of the blow!
Row or the squall'll twist her
Broadside on to it!—*Row!*

The rest will be two reef sailing. . . . . . .
That was a night indeed !

Printed in Great Britain

SONG OF THE RED WAR-BOAT

Heark'ee, Thor of the Thunder!
We are not here for a jest—
For wager, warfare, or plunder,
Or to put your power to test.
This work is none of our wishing—
We would house at home if we might—
But our master is wrecked out fishing.
We go to find him to-night.

For we hold that in all disaster—
As the Gods Themselves have said—
A Man must stand by his Master
Till one of the two is dead.

That is our way of thinking,
Now you can do as you will,
While we try to save her from sinking
And hold her head to it still.
Bale her and keep her moving,
Or she'll break her back in the trough . . . .
Who said the weather's improving,
Or the swells are taking off?

Sodden, and chafed and aching,
Gone in the loins and knees—
No matter—the day is breaking,
And there's far less weight to the seas!

Up mast, and finish baling—
In oars, and out with the mead—
The rest will be two-reef sailing . . . .
That was a night indeed!

But we hold that in all disaster
(*And faith, we have found it true!*)
If only you stand by your Master,
The Gods will stand by you!

THE SEA AND THE HILLS

THE SEA AND THE HILLS

Who hath desired the Sea?—the sight of salt water unbounded—
The heave and the halt and the hurl, and the crash of the comber wind-hounded?
The sleek-barrelled swell before storm, grey, foamless, enormous, and growing—
Stark calm on the lap of the Line or the crazy-eyed hurricane blowing—
His Sea in no showing the same—his Sea and the same 'neath each showing—
His Sea as she slackens or thrills?
So and no otherwise—so and no otherwise—hillmen desire their Hills!

Who hath desired the Sea?—the immense and contemptuous surges?
The shudder, the stumble, the swerve, as the star-stabbing bowsprit emerges?
The orderly clouds of the Trades, and the ridged, roaring sapphire thereunder—
Unheralded cliff-haunting flaws and the headsail's low-volleying thunder—
His Sea in no wonder the same—his Sea and the same through each wonder:
His Sea as she rages or stills?
So and no otherwise—so and no otherwise—hillmen desire their Hills.

Who hath desired the Sea? Her menaces swift as her mercies,
The in-rolling walls of the fog and the silver-winged breeze that disperses?
The unstable mined berg going South and the calvings and groans that declare it;
White water half-guessed overside and the moon breaking timely to bare it;
His Sea as his fathers have dared—his Sea as his children shall dare it—
His Sea as she serves him or kills?
So and no otherwise—so and no otherwise—hillmen desire their Hills.

Who hath desired the Sea?—the sight of salt water
unbounded—
The heave and the halt and the hurl, and the crash
of the comber wind-hounded?

Printed in Great Britain

THE SEA AND THE HILLS

Who hath desired the Sea? Her excellent loneliness
rather
Than forecourts of kings, and her outermost pits than
the streets where men gather
Inland, among dust, under trees—inland where the
slayer may slay him
Inland, out of reach of her arms, and the bosom whereon
he must lay him—
His Sea at the first that betrayed—at the last that shall
never betray him—
His Sea that his being fulfils?
So and no otherwise—so and no otherwise—hillmen
desire their Hills.

FRANKIE'S TRADE

FRANKIE'S TRADE

Old Horn to All Atlantic said:
    (*A-hay O! To me O!*)
'Now where did Frankie learn his trade?
For he ran me down with a three-reef mains'le.'
    (*All round the Horn!*)

Atlantic answered:—'Not from me!
You better ask the cold North Sea,
For he ran me down under all plain canvas.'
    (*All round the Horn!*)

The North Sea answered:—'He's my man,
For he came to me when he began—
Frankie Drake in an open coaster.
(*All round the Sands!*)

'I caught him young and I used him sore,
So you never shall startle Frankie more,
Without capsizing Earth and her waters.
(*All round the Sands!*)

'I did not favour him at all.
I made him pull and I made him haul—
And stand his trick with the common sailors.
(*All round the Sands!*)

'I froze him stiff and I fogged him blind,
And kicked him home with his road to find
By what he could see in a three-day snow-storm.
(*All round the Sands!*)

'I learned him his trade o' winter nights,
'Twixt Mardyk Fort and Dunkirk lights
On a five-knot tide with the forts a-firing.
(*All round the Sands!*)

"I learned him his trade o' winter nights,
'Twixt Mardyk Fort and Dunkirk lights,
On a five-knot tide with the forts a-firing.

Printed in Great Britain

FRANKIE'S TRADE

'Before his beard began to shoot,
I showed him the length of the Spaniard's foot—
And I reckon he clapped the boot on it later.
(*All round the Sands!*)

'If there's a risk which you can make,
That's worse than he was used to take
Nigh every week in the way of his business;
(*All round the Sands!*)

'If there's a trick that you can try,
Which he hasn't met in time gone by,
Not once or twice, but ten times over;
(*All round the Sands!*)

'If you can teach him aught that's new,
(*A-hay O! To me O!*)
I'll give you Bruges and Niewport too,
And the ten tall churches that stand between 'em,'
Storm along my gallant Captains!
(*All round the Horn!*)

THE SCHOLARS

"Some hundreds of the younger Naval Officers, whose education was interrupted by the War are now to be sent to various Colleges at Cambridge to continue their studies. The experiment will be watched with great interest." *Daily Papers* (1919).

THE SCHOLARS

"*Oh, show me how a rose can shut and be a bud again!*"
Nay, watch my Lords of the Admiralty, for they have
the work in train.
They have taken the men that were careless lads at
Dartmouth in 'Fourteen.
And entered them in the landward schools as though
no war had been.

They have piped the children off all the seas from the Falklands to the Bight,
And quartered them on the Colleges to learn to read and write!

Their books were rain and sleet and fog—the dry gale and the snow.
Their teachers were the hornéd mines and the hump-backed Death below.
Their schools were walled by the walking mists and roofed by the waiting skies
When they conned their task in a new-sown field with the Moonlight Sacrifice.
They were not rated too young to teach, not reckoned unfit to guide
When they formed their class on Helle's beach at the bows of the "River Clyde."
Their eyes are sunk by endless watch, their faces roughed by the spray,
Their feet are drawn by the wet sea-boots they changed not night or day
When they guarded the six-knot convoy's flank on the road to Norroway.

Their books were rain and sleet and fog—the dry gale and the snow.
Their teachers were the hornéd mines and the hump-backed Death below.

Printed in Great Britain

THE SCHOLARS

Their ears are stuffed with the week-long roar of the
West-Atlantic gale
When the sloops were watching the Irish Shore from
Galway to Kinsale.
Their hands are scored where the life-lines cut, or the
dripping funnel-stays
When they followed their leader at thirty knots between
The Skaw and The Naze.
Their mouths are filled with the magic words they
learned at the collier's hatch
When they coaled in the foul December dawns and
sailed in the forenoon-watch.
(Or measured the weight of a Pentland tide and the
wind off Ronaldshay,
Till the target mastered the breathless tug and the
hawser carried away.)
They know the price to be paid for a fault—for a
gauge-clock wrongly read,
Or a picket-boat to the gangway brought bows-on and
full-ahead,
Or the drowsy second's lack of thought that costs a
dozen dead.

They have touched a knowledge outreaching speech —as when the cutters were sent
To harvest the dreadful mile of beach after the "Vanguard" went.
They have learned great faith and little fear and a high heart in distress,
And how to suffer each sodden year of heaped-up weariness.
They have borne the bridle upon their lips and the yoke upon their neck
Since they went down to the sea in ships to save a world from wreck—
Since the chests were slung down the college stair at Dartmouth in 'Fourteen;
And now they are quit of the sea-affair as though no war had been.
Far have they steamed and much have they known, and most would they fain forget,
But now they are come to their joyous own with all the world in their debt.

* * * * *

Hallowed River, most gracious Trees, Chapel beyond compare,
Here be gentlemen tired of the seas—take them into your care.

Far have they come, much have they braved. Give
    them their hour of play,
While the hidden things their hands have saved work
    for them day by day.
Till the grateful Past their youth redeemed return
    them their youth once more,
And the Soul of the Child at last lets fall the unjust
    load that it bore.